SUPER
CHEF

The Cooking of
FRANCE

This book is dedicated to the
people of New York City.

This author's sincere gratitude to Peter Mavrikis, Michelle Bisson, Kay Petronio, and Anahid Hamparian.

Published by Marshall Cavendish Benchmark
An imprint of Marshall Cavendish Corporation
All rights reserved.

Website: www.marshallcavendish.us

Text © 2012 by Matthew Locricchio

Food photographs © 2012 Jack McConnell, McConnell, McNamara & Company
Map © 2012 by Mike Reagan
Illustrations by Janet Hamlin
Illustrations © 2012 by Marshall Cavendish Corporation

This publication represents the opinions and views of the author based on Matthew Locricchio's personal experience, knowledge, and research. The information in this book serves as a general guide only. The author and publisher have used their best efforts in preparing this book and disclaim liability rising directly and indirectly from the use and application of this book.

Other Marshall Cavendish Offices:
Marshall Cavendish International (Asia) Private Limited, 1 New Industrial Road, Singapore 536196 • Marshall Cavendish International (Thailand) Co Ltd. 253 Asoke, 12th Flr, Sukhumvit 21 Road, Klongtoey Nua, Wattana, Bangkok 10110, Thailand • Marshall Cavendish (Malaysia) Sdn Bhd, Times Subang, Lot 46, Subang Hi-Tech Industrial Park, Batu Tiga, 40000 Shah Alam, Selangor Darul Ehsan, Malaysia

Marshall Cavendish is a trademark of Times Publishing Limited
All websites were available and accurate when this book was sent to press.

Library of Congress Cataloging-in-Publication Data

Locricchio, Matthew.
   The cooking of France / Matthew Locricchio.
       p. cm. — (Superchef—2nd ed.)
   Summary: "Introduces the different culinary regions of France and presents many kinds of recipes for traditional French dishes"— Provided by publisher.
   Includes bibliographical references and index.
   ISBN 978-1-60870-551-1 (print) — ISBN 978-1-60870-739-3 (ebook)
1. Cooking, French—Juvenile literature. 2. Food habits—France—Juvenile literature. I. Title.
   TX719.L62 2012
   641.5944—dc22
       2010052549

Editor: Peter Mavrikis
Publisher: Michelle Bisson
Art Director: Anahid Hamparian
Series design by Kay Petronio
Art direction for food photography by Matthew Locricchio
Food styling by Marie Hirschfeld and Matthew Locricchio

Photo Credits: Robert Harding Picture Library/Superstock: 14; Yoshio Tomii/Superstock: 16; Steve Vidler/Superstock: 19; Matthew Locricchio: 51; Photka/Fotolia: 90; Volff/Fotolia: 91; Le Do/Fotolia: 91; Rimglow/Fotolia: 92; Peter Jameson: 96.

Printed in Malaysia (T)
135642

SUPER
CHEF

The Cooking of
FRANCE

second edition
Matthew Locricchio

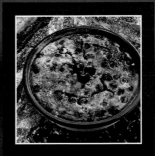

with photos by Jack McConnell

mc **Marshall Cavendish**
Benchmark

New York

Contents

Desserts   80

Dear Reader,

I can't think of a better way to learn about a culture first-hand than to cook and savor its cuisine. Understanding the breadth of Italian pasta varieties, or Greek phyllo specialties and greens dishes, of Chinese dumplings, Indian curries, Thai spice blends, and more helps us understand something about the geography, history, and soul of a country.

My first memories of food come from my own family, of Sunday meals that lasted half the day and holidays that required a week of cooking. There was a rhythm to the dishes we ate depending on the time of year, with specific sweets for Christmas, breads for New Year's, and the vegan fare my grandmother would prepare as we fasted for Easter. For me, food became synonymous with both communicating and sharing. The dinner table was a time of talking about the issues of the day. The holidays and impromptu visits by family and friends became reason to put a little something on the table for others to enjoy. Those are important lessons to carry through life and they are learned young. As a kid I always helped in the kitchen, regardless of whether I wanted to or not! Thanks to that I learned to cook fairly young, and by the time I was a teenager, I was inviting my friends over to try my own creations.

Young people today are much more food savvy than I was way back in the 1960s and 1970s. Teenagers have a much broader experience with ethnic foods than I ever did. There was no such thing as organic food when I was growing up. We also did not have access to the constant stream of information available today. Ironically, with the overabundance of information out there on food, there is very little real knowledge about how to cook simple, healthy, good food.

The Superchef series of cookbooks aims to do just that and in the process show young people that the world is, indeed, one delicious kitchen where many different cooking traditions flourish.

Cooking is an art, but it's also more than that. People can live without music, paintings, sculpture, and literature, but we can't live without food! So, enjoy the process, but better yet, enjoy sharing it with others.

Diane Kochilas

Consulting chef
Pylos Restaurant, NYC

Diane Kochilas is a chef, author, and teacher. She has published over a dozen cookbooks including, *The Food and Wine of Greece*, *The Greek Vegetarian*, *Meze*, *The Glorious Foods of Greece*, *Mediterranean Grilling* and more. Diane has also made numerous television and radio appearances, and runs a cooking school focusing on traditional Greek recipes, as well as the culture of Greece. To learn more about Diane, go to www.dianekochilas.com.

From the Author

Welcome to the second edition of Superchef. When we first created this series of cookbooks our goal was to introduce new cooks to traditional yet tantalizing recipes from around the world, adapted to work in your kitchen. That goal has not changed.

Young chefs like yourself who discovered Superchef have been learning to cook international recipes with family and friends ever since. The world of satisfying recipes, along with the basic principles of kitchen safety, food handling, and common-sense nutrition is what made Superchef so popular when it was first introduced. Those same goals hold true with the new edition.

Learning to master authentic international recipes and sharing them with family and friends is the motivation behind these cookbooks. This edition offers the invitation to new cooks as well as old to step into the kitchen and start cooking. Within this complete series you will find classic recipes from eight different countries. The recipes are not necessarily all low-fat or low-calorie, but they are all healthful. Even if you are a vegetarian, you will find recipes without meat or with suggestions to make the dish meatless.

Superchef can change the way you feel about cooking. You can learn to make authentic and delicious dishes from recipes that have been tested by young cooks in kitchens like yours. The recipes range from very basic to challenging. The instructions take you through the preparation of each dish step by step. Once you learn the basic techniques of the recipes, you will understand the principles of cooking fresh food successfully.

There is no better way to get to know people than to share a meal with them. Today, more than ever, it is essential to understand the many cultures that inhabit our planet. One way to really learn about a country is to know how its food tastes. Cooking is the one thing we all have in common. You can prepare a recipe in your kitchen and know that somewhere, perhaps many thousands of miles away, that same dish is probably being prepared in the country where it originated.

Every day in the United States we are reminded of our multicultural richness just by the foods available to us. The delicious result of that abundance is that American cooking has developed into one of the most diverse and appealing cuisines on the planet.

Learning to cook is one of the most important things anybody can do. Cooking skills stay with you your entire life and it sure is fun. Learning to cook takes practice, patience, and common sense, but it's not nuclear science. Cooking certainly has its rewards. Just the simple act of preparing food can lift your spirits. Nothing brings family and friends together better than cooking and then sharing the meal you've made. It can be fun, and you get to eat your mistakes. It can even lead to a high-paying career. Most importantly, you can be proud to say, "Oh, glad you liked it. I did it myself."

Happy cooking!

Matthew Locricchio

Before You Begin

A Word about Safety

Safety and common sense are the two most important ingredients in any recipe. Before you begin to make the recipes in this book, take a few minutes to master some simple kitchen safety rules.

Ask an adult to be your assistant chef. To ensure your safety, some steps in a recipe are best done with the help of an adult, like handling pots of boiling water or hot cooking oils. Good cooking is about teamwork. With an adult assistant to help, you've got the makings of a perfect team.

Read the entire recipe before you start to prepare it, and have a clear understanding of how the recipe works. If something is not clear, ask your teammate to explain it.

Dress the part of a chef. Wear an apron. Tie back long hair so that it's out of your food and away from open flames. Why not do what a chef does and wear a clean hat to cover your hair!

Always start with clean hands and a clean kitchen before you begin any recipe. Always wash your hands again after handling raw meat, poultry, or fish. Leave the kitchen clean when you're done.

Pot holders and hot pads are your friends. The hands they save may be your own. Use them only if they are dry. Using wet holders on a hot pot can cause a serious burn!

Keep the handles of the pots and pans turned toward the middle of the stove. That way you won't accidentally hit them and knock over pots of hot food. Always use pot holders to open or move a pan on the stove or in the oven.

● **Remember to turn off the stove and oven when you are finished cooking.** Sounds like a simple idea, but it's easy to forget.

Be Sharp about Knives

● A simple rule about knife safety is that your hands work as a team. One hand grips the handle and operates the knife while the other guides the food you are cutting. The hand holding the food should never come close to the blade of the knife. Keep the fingertips that hold the food slightly curved and out of the path of the blade, and use your thumb to keep the food steady. Go slowly. There is no reason to rush.

● Always hold the knife handle with dry hands. If your hands are wet, the knife might slip.

● Work on a cutting board, never a tabletop or countertop.

● Never place sharp knives in a sink full of soapy water, where they could be hidden from view. Someone reaching into the water might get hurt.

French cooking is real cooking. The time spent preparing a meal is rewarded with wonderful results—delicious deep flavor and exciting dishes. The French don't just cook for the sake of having something to eat. They prepare food because they love food. French cooking is a combination of things: one part excellent ingredients, one part patience, one part technique, and one part cooking magic. Many professional chefs learn to cook using basic French techniques. Once you learn a few simple skills, you'll know why this cuisine is so highly regarded.

Blanch

To plunge vegetables into a pot of boiling water for a minute or two to lightly cook them and help keep their color from fading.

Fold

To gently blend lighter ingredients with heavier ones so that they are not overmixed.

Reduce

To boil a liquid at a high temperature until it has partly evaporated. The technique of reducing is used to thicken sauces without the addition of fats or flour.

Sauté

To lightly fry food in a small amount of fat, butter, or oil, while stirring with a spoon or spatula.

Simmer

To cook food in a liquid at just below the boiling point. Gentle bubbles roll lazily to the top of the liquid that is simmering. The technique of simmering brings out maximum flavor and is used frequently in French cooking.

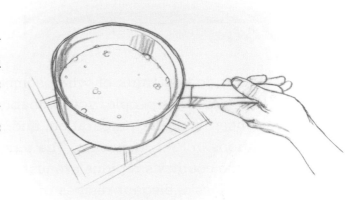

Skim

Fats or impurities will rise to the surface of simmering or boiling soups and sauces. Skimming removes these unwanted residues while also reducing fat and enriching flavor. Use a large metal spoon or small ladle to scoop off the top layer.

The Regions of France and How They Taste

What do you think of when someone mentions French cooking? If you are like most people, you probably think of elaborate cuisine with rich sauces, complex preparation, and precise recipes. But there are two traditions in French cuisine. The unique flavors and cooking styles of each of the country's regions are just as much a part of the food of France as the classic, elegant recipes of centuries past. Regional cooking is many things. It is the cooking of farmers and fishermen, of grandmothers passing on recipes to the younger generation, as well as the recipes of new young chefs. In this book, we will explore the regional side of French cooking, with a few detours along the way.

France, located at the center of western Europe, is the Continent's third-largest country. It is a land of impressive natural surroundings, complete with the dramatic towering Alps in the east, ancient white chalk cliffs along the coastline of Normandy, and hillsides covered with grapevines and olive trees along the shores of the Mediterranean Sea. As you travel through its unique countryside, the many different accents of the people remind you of France's great cultural diversity. In Alsace, you hear French spoken with a German accent; in Brittany, Celtic; and in Provence, Italian. But in spite of the cultural influences in the different regions, the people and the food are definitely all French.

The French consider food one of life's greatest pleasures. Regional recipes, their ingredients, and the origins of these ingredients, including how vegetables and herbs were grown, are an essential part of French life. So is sharing food with family and friends. Most important, however, is the simple question, "How does it taste?" Because it is the sumptuous taste of French cooking that sets it apart from the rest of the world's cuisine. Many people consider the cooking of France to be the finest in the world. Words like "spectacular," "elegant," "outrageous," and "richly delicious" are all used to describe the experience of eating the food of France. It seems the whole world loves what comes out of the French kitchen.

The idea that the French eat nothing but rich food, high in fat and loaded with calories, is simply not true. Not every dish served at a typical French meal is very rich. That is important to keep in mind when you plan a menu from this book. Some rich foods are meant to be eaten on special occasions, while other, lighter dishes are better suited to everyday dining.

Traditionally, French cooking is divided into at least eleven culinary regions, and the food of each of these regions is as different and distinctive as its people. For the purposes of this book, however, we have divided the food of France into three regions—the north, the central region, and the south. The cooking of each of these larger regions has special characteristics that reflect its unique landscape, climate, flavors, and traditions.

The North

This region is regarded by many as the heartland of French cuisine because it is here that so much of French cooking has its roots. We begin in the historic province of Brittany, surrounded on three sides by the Atlantic, where one discovers a land of contrasts. The jagged coastline, regarded as one of the most treacherous in the world, also has many natural harbors that provide shelter from the sea for both fishermen and vacationers. This entire region, once covered with forests, was home to Celtic settlers who came from Britain about

An ornate drinking fountain and cafés in Concarneau, Brittany.

fifteen hundred years ago. In some parts of Brittany, people still speak an ancient Celtic language called Breton.

The sea dominates much of the life along Brittany's coast. The local farmers fertilize their vegetables with seaweed, which adds wonderful flavor. As you move inland, you discover small, quaint houses and large expanses of farms, fields, and tiny villages, where the scent of sea air is a familiar part of daily life. Temperatures are usually moderate and ideal for farming spinach, carrots, potatoes, cauliflower, and cabbage, all of which are popular in local recipes.

Farther north, along the coastline of the English Channel, is the province of Normandy, home to the city of Boulogne. One of Europe's unsurpassed sources for fresh fish, Boulogne is the largest fishing port in France. Turbot, monkfish, scallops, sole, lobster, and herring are fished from the waters off Normandy. In from the coast, more than 8 million apple trees cover the countryside. There are also lush pastures with grazing animals and farms filled with vegetables. This is truly a province of bounty and captivating beauty.

The world-famous apples that grow in Normandy find their way into legendary French recipes. The richest cream and the finest butter, cheeses, and eggs are also an important part of Normandy's culinary history. The phrase *à la normande* added to a recipe generally means it is prepared with a sauce enriched with cream and flavored with apple cider.

It is, however, the northern province of Île-de-France, home to the famous city of Paris, that most people think of as the food capital of France, and even of the world. The rich soil of the province's countryside produces some of the best fruits and vegetables in France. East of Île-de-France, the lush pastures of the province of Champagne produce not only the most famous wine in the world but also Brie, a rich and creamy soft cheese. Strawberries, peaches, grapes, pears, peas, and almonds all thrive in this area's moderate climate.

Paris benefits from the many regional specialties of Champagne and Île-de-France. Local meats, seafood, and vegetables find their way into the city's legendary restaurants and home kitchens, too. The variety of food in Paris is remarkable. One can choose from elegant establishments serving classic French cuisine or simple cafés and bistros serving specialties like onion soup and *croque-monsieur* (a crunchy ham and cheese sandwich). Bakeries called *patisseries* create thousands of delectable cakes, tarts, and cream puffs each day. The hardest part for the visitor is choosing which pastry to enjoy—a delightful chore!

If you travel far to the east of Paris, through the province of Lorraine and almost to the German border, you will see the grasslands of Alsace province. Here is more fertile farmland, rich with grains and fruits. Alsace lies in a narrow ribbon that stretches from the Swiss border in the south to the German border in the north, nestled between the Vosges Mountains and the Rhine River. The Alsatians have prepared some of France's most treasured cooking since the Middle Ages. The food of their province is hearty and outstanding. Their most famous dish is quiche Lorraine, a rich medley of eggs, cream, and cheese baked to perfection in a pastry shell.

For a taste of the north try: Chicken with Apples and Cream; French Onion Soup; Bacon and Egg Custard Tart; Cheese Soufflé; and Ham and Cheese Crunches.

The Central Region

Burgundy, Lyonnais, and Franche-Comté provinces are part of another region where exceptional French cooking has well-established foundations. Many food historians believe that the central region, rather than the north, is the real heart of French cooking. More importantly, French culture and history have survived here longer than anywhere else in France and, as a result, the region's culinary roots grow deep.

Lyon, the third-largest city in France, is located in Lyonnais province, at just the right spot for perfect food. Close by are the legendary *poulardes*

Saint Georges footbridge in Lyon offers a perfect spot to experience the beauty of this historic city in central France.

de Bresse—the fattened chickens of the tiny province of Bresse—regarded by many as the finest in the world. Each chicken roams the spacious, grassy hillsides and eats a feed composed of milk and corn. To the north are the famous freshwater breeding ponds of Dombes. These ponds date back to the twelfth century and provide some 2,000 tons of freshwater fish a year for European kitchens and markets. The Rhône and Saône rivers also wind their way through the central region and provide additional fresh fish. Wild mushrooms from the region's forests add their share of attractive flavors to many recipes. The fruits and vegetables here are superb and plentiful. The mustard from Dijon, the sausages and world-famous chocolate from Lyon, and the cured hams of the Morvan Plateau help to define this region as the gastronomic center of France.

The Alps, which border the central region on the east, attract countless tourists each year, not only to ski but also to enjoy the area's cooking. This is dairy country, and in the historic province of Dauphiné, milk and cheese are blended with potatoes to create rich scalloped potatoes. Gruyère, from Franche-Comté at the foothills of a mountain range north of the Alps, has long been a household name in fine cheese. If you visit the region of Franche-Comté you are likely to have walnut oil used to dress your salad as olive oil, because of the abundance of walnut trees that grow in region. A popular savory appetizer in the Burgundy region is a tantalizing cheese puff with melt-in-your mouth goodness. The puffs are rich and satisfying, yet still light to the taste. The pastry for the cheese puffs is the same used to make the legendary dessert cream puffs with ice cream and chocolate sauce. The recipe is just another example of how versatile French cooking can be.

To the northwest, along the banks of the Loire River, you will see legendary castles that once housed the kings and queens of France. In the Loire Valley, called the "garden of France," are the provinces of Touraine and Anjou. The fruits and vegetables cultivated here are of the highest quality. Strawberries and cherries, plums and table grapes abound. These are not only eaten fresh but are also made into delicious preserves and jellies. Carrots, leeks, potatoes, onions, and tomatoes appear as the first vegetables of the season, a welcome sight in markets and restaurants throughout France.

The famous "mushrooms of Paris" are actually grown here in the Loire Valley, in natural underground caves in the town of Saumur. France has close to 500 miles (800 kilometers) of underground workings, making it the third-largest producer of fresh mushrooms in the world. With such an abundance of exceptional ingredients, as well as its long history, it is easy to understand why central France is valued for its part in French cuisine.

For a taste of central France try: Tossed Salad with Cheese Croutons; Cheese Puffs; Roast Chicken; Scalloped Potatoes; Roast Pork with Dried Plums; Glazed Carrots; and Cream Puffs with Ice Cream and Chocolate Sauce.

The South

The magic of the south, especially the region of Provence, has drawn painters, poets, tourists, and food lovers for countless years. Here are black cypress trees growing out of red soil, spectacular hills formed from jagged rocks, and olive groves brimming with ripening black and green fruit, their silvery leaves shining in the hot sun. Fields of fragrant purple and green herbs and endless varieties of vegetables grow in colorful rows everywhere. It is no wonder the south of France is paradise to food lovers and cooks alike.

The glistening waters of the Mediterranean lie to the south, adding to the beauty and popularity of Provence. Everything about this province is unique. The brilliant sunlight is remarkable, the sound of the powerful north wind is haunting, and the cooking is as exciting as the land itself.

Olives and grapes thrive here, as does wheat in the higher elevations. The province produces an abundance of fruits, vegetables, olives, and olive oil. The local cooks know how to create exciting cuisine that is rich with color, flavor, freshness, and delicate fragrance. In the adjoining province of Languedoc, Roquefort cheese, mussels, anchovies, and turbot all find their way into the local dishes. The cooking of Languedoc shows the influence of nearby Spain in its variety and bold combinations of ingredients.

It is the cooking of Provence, however, that remains the most famous of the southern region. Dishes that use the finest local ingredients remain the favorites of local diners and tourists alike. Vegetables are combined in a carefully cooked casserole to become ratatouille. Cherries appear in appealing seasonal cakes. Beef stews bring together the best of fresh ingredients in tasty dishes that are enjoyed both hot and cold.

Salads are a treasured part of Provençal cooking, too. The markets here overflow with lettuces, tomatoes, potatoes, green beans, peppers, and artichokes. Olives grown on massive old trees in the port city of Nice,

The fragrance, color, and selection of this fruit market in Aux Airs, Povence, attracts early morning shoppers.

just south of Provence, are the source of the delicate olive oil essential to local recipes. The herbs of Provence also add distinctive flavor to regional recipes. These include thyme, rosemary, tarragon, bay leaves, basil, garlic, and oregano. Even when these herbs have been dried, they still burst with flavor and aroma.

For a taste of the south of France try: Combination Salad; Potato and Leek Soup; Turbot with Fresh Vegetables; Beef Stew with Tomatoes and Olives; Vegetable Casserole; Scallops in Cream Sauce; and Cherry Cake.

There is much to discover about French cooking and even more to taste and enjoy. Now that you have some idea of what makes French cuisine so legendary, it is time to prepare the dishes that have the whole world saying, *"Ah, magnifique!"*

Soups, Salads, and Breads

Combination salad.

Chicken Stock
Fond Blanc de Volaille

There is nothing that can compare with the flavor of homemade chicken stock. It is easy to make, so you can always have it on hand when you need it. You can buy canned or frozen stock and still get good flavor, but using homemade is the best way to control the amount of salt in any recipe using chicken stock. This recipe will introduce you to a *bouquet garni*, a tiny bundle of herbs and spices that the French use to flavor their dishes.

Serves 6

Ingredients

STOCK

1 whole chicken or chicken parts, wings or legs
  (3 to 3 ½ pounds)

1 medium-size onion

2 carrots

2 stalks celery

3 quarts cold water

1 ½ teaspoons salt

BOUQUET GARNI

5- to 6-inch square cheesecloth

3 sprigs fresh flat-leaf parsley

1 bay leaf

3 or 4 black peppercorns

2 or 3 thyme sprigs

cotton string

On your mark, get set . . .

- Rinse the chicken and place it in a large stockpot.

- Chop the onion (no need to peel it), carrots, and celery, and add them to the pot.

- To make the bouquet garni: Lay the cheesecloth square on a clean work surface. Place all the ingredients for the bouquet inside the square, tie it into a bundle with the string at the top, and place it in the pot. If you make the string long enough, you can tie the bundle to the handle of the pot, which makes it really easy to remove at the end of the cooking.

Cook!

- Add the cold water and salt to the pot, and bring to a boil on medium-high heat. As the liquid comes to a boil, use a large spoon to skim off any foam or impurities that rise to the surface. Reduce the heat to low, partially cover, and simmer the stock for 1 ½ hours.

- Get an adult to help you remove the pot from the heat and drain the stock into a colander lined with cheesecloth and placed over a large heatproof bowl or pot. Gently press on the ingredients to extract the flavor.

- When the cooked ingredients are cool enough to handle, discard the vegetables and the bouquet garni. The chicken in this recipe can be removed from the bone after it is cooked and used cold in salads or for delicious sandwiches.

- Cool the stock for 20 minutes, then cover and fully chill in the refrigerator for at least a few hours, and remove any fat that has risen to the top of the stock. If you are using the stock immediately, skim the fat at the top with a large spoon and discard. The stock will keep in the refrigerator for 4 days or frozen for 3 months.

French Onion Soup
Soupe à l'Oignon Gratinée

The story goes that one of France's most famous chefs created this soup in the fourteenth century, hoping to please the king. And that is just what he did! As you prepare this most famous of all French soups, the wonderful aroma of onions gently cooking in butter will fill your kitchen. Try making it with homemade chicken stock (page 22). Served with French bread (page 34), it becomes a complete meal. To make this recipe vegetarian, substitute vegetable stock for the chicken or beef stock.

Serves 6

Ingredients

4 medium-size onions (about 2 pounds)

4 tablespoons butter

1 teaspoon salt

4 cups homemade chicken stock or canned low-sodium chicken, beef, or vegetable broth

1 tablespoon flour

freshly ground black pepper to taste

6 slices French or Italian bread, ½ inch thick

1 ½ cups Gruyère or Parmesan cheese (about 6 ounces)

On your mark, get set . . .

- Peel the onions and cut them into ½-inch slices. Measure 6 cups and set aside.

- You will need 6 individual ovenproof soup bowls that can go under the broiler or a large ovenproof casserole, which will work just as well.

Cook!

- Melt the butter in a 6-quart heavy-bottomed pan on low heat.

- Add the onion slices and salt, and cook for 20 minutes with the pan partially covered. Remove the lid and continue to cook until the onions caramelize to a soft brown color. It is not necessary to stir the onions constantly. Every so often, give them a stir and check to make sure they are not burning; if so, reduce the heat a little.

- Toward the end of the cooking time, bring the stock to a simmer on low heat.

- After the onions have changed color and are very limp, sprinkle on the flour and mix in well. Continue to cook for another minute or so.

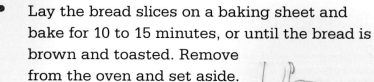

- Add the onions to the simmering stock and raise the heat to medium. Add the pepper and bring to a boil.

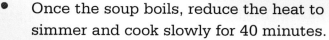

- Once the soup boils, reduce the heat to simmer and cook slowly for 40 minutes.

- Preheat the oven to 400°F.

- Lay the bread slices on a baking sheet and bake for 10 to 15 minutes, or until the bread is brown and toasted. Remove from the oven and set aside.

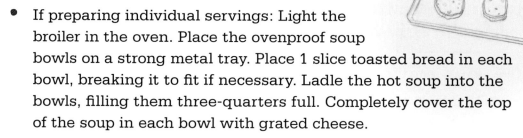

- Grate the cheese, measure 1 ½ cups, and set aside.

- If preparing individual servings: Light the broiler in the oven. Place the ovenproof soup bowls on a strong metal tray. Place 1 slice toasted bread in each bowl, breaking it to fit if necessary. Ladle the hot soup into the bowls, filling them three-quarters full. Completely cover the top of the soup in each bowl with grated cheese.

- Have an adult assistant help you place the bowls under the broiler, and broil for about 3 minutes. The cheese will melt and become bubbly and golden brown. Keep a close watch on it so it doesn't burn.

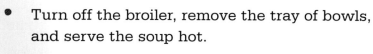

- Turn off the broiler, remove the tray of bowls, and serve the soup hot.

- If using a large casserole: Place the toasted bread in the bottom of the ovenproof casserole. Add the soup. Cover the top of the casserole with the grated cheese.

- Bake for 10 minutes at 400°F. Turn the oven to broil and melt and brown the cheese. This will take 3 to 4 minutes. Keep a close watch on it so it doesn't burn.

- Turn off the broiler. Remove the casserole from the oven and serve hot.

Chef's Tip

If making the soup ahead of time, prepare the soup, let it cool, and refrigerate it. When you are ready to serve the soup, gently reheat it on low heat, assemble with the bread and cheese, and bake/broil as directed on pages 25-27.

Potato and Leek Soup
Potage Parmentier

This traditional French recipe is as simple as it is versatile. Once pureed, it can be served hot as potato and leek soup, *potage parmentier*. Or you can chill it after it is pureed and serve it with fresh chopped chives, and it becomes *crème vichyssoise*. What happens if you want to make it but you have no leeks? That's easy. Just substitute onions and you can enjoy a really delicious potato and onion soup called *potage soubise*. So that means this easy recipe is three soups in one.

Serves 6

Ingredients

5 medium-size leeks (about 1 pound) or
   1 pound yellow onions

3 Idaho potatoes

7 cups water

2 teaspoons salt

⅓ cup heavy cream (optional)

chopped fresh flat-leaf parsley or
   fresh chives for garnish

On your mark, get set . . .

- Cut off the root ends of the leeks and discard. Cut away any leaves that are discolored or wilted. Cut off most of the green tops, leaving about 1 inch of green and all the white bottom. You will end up with leeks about 6 inches long.

- Lay each leek flat on a cutting board and, using a sharp knife, start at the white end and split the leek in half lengthwise, cutting it into two long pieces.

- Rinse the leeks very well under cold running water to remove any sand that might be trapped in the layers of the leaves. Gently lift and separate the sections as you wash them to remove all the sand.

- Cut the leeks crosswise into thin slices and measure about 3 cups.

- If you are using onions instead of leeks, peel and cut the onions in half and then into thin slices and measure 3 cups.

- Peel and cut the potatoes into small cubes and measure 4 cups.

Cook!

- Combine the leeks (or onions), potatoes, water, and salt in a large pot. Bring to a boil. This will take about 15 minutes.

- Cover the pot with a lid slightly ajar, reduce the heat to simmer, and cook for 35 to 40 minutes, or until the vegetables are very tender. Taste the soup and add extra salt if needed.

- Using a soup ladle or potato masher, gently mash the potatoes and leeks to lightly thicken and puree the soup.

- If you are adding the cream, add it just before serving and make sure the soup is off the heat, or it may separate.

- Serve hot, garnished with the chopped parsley or chives.

Chef's Tip

If serving the soup cold, don't add the cream until you have completely chilled the soup and are ready to serve it. Garnish with the chopped chives or parsley.

Combination Salad
Salade Niçoise

This famous salad is from Nice, located in the south of France on the Mediterranean shore. The ingredients of this salad are dressed separately with a Dijon mustard dressing. Look for the freshest ingredients when shopping for this salad, and serve it with French bread (page 34) for a great summertime lunch or supper. To make this salad vegetarian, simply omit the tuna.

Serves 6

Ingredients

DRESSING

½ cup extra-virgin olive oil

1 tablespoon red wine vinegar

1 tablespoon fresh lemon juice

1 tablespoon Dijon mustard

1 tablespoon chopped fresh flat-leaf parsley or fresh chives

¼ teaspoon dry mustard

freshly ground black pepper to taste

SALAD

1 head Boston lettuce

8 to 10 red-skin, Yukon gold, or other small potatoes (golf-ball size)

½ pound fresh green beans

6 to 8 Niçoise or pitted black olives

2 ripe tomatoes

3 eggs

1 can (6 ounces) oil-packed tuna

On your mark, get set . . .

- Place all the ingredients for the dressing in a glass jar with a lid and shake well to combine. Set aside.

- Wash the lettuce leaves and pat or spin dry. Wrap the lettuce in paper towels to absorb any excess water and refrigerate.

- Rinse and scrub the potatoes to remove any dirt.

- Rinse the green beans. Snap off the stem end of each bean and pull it down to remove any string.

- Count the olives and set aside.

- Wash the tomatoes and remove the stem ends. Cut the tomatoes into quarters.

Cook!

- Bring a 3-quart pan of salted water to a boil. Drop in the green beans and cook for 5 to 6 minutes, or until tender but still a little crunchy when you bite one.

- Drain the beans and flood with cold running water to stop the cooking. Cut the beans in half and set aside.

- Place the eggs in a small pan of water and bring to a boil. Reduce the heat to simmer and cook for 12 minutes.

- In the meantime, prepare the potatoes: Bring a 3-quart pan of salted water to a boil. Add the potatoes and cook for 10 to 12 minutes, or until they feel tender when pierced with the tip of a knife.

- Drain the potatoes and return them to the pan for 1 or 2 minutes to absorb any excess cooking liquid. Remove the potatoes from the heat and set aside to cool.

- When the eggs have finished cooking, place the pan in the sink and flood the eggs with cold running water for 1 minute. Allow the eggs to cool in the cold water.

- Peel the eggs under gently running cold water. Set the eggs aside.

- Once the potatoes are cool enough to handle, slice them into ¼-inch slices.

- Place the potatoes, green beans, tomatoes, and 1 ½ tablespoons of the dressing in a large bowl; remember to shake the dressing again before measuring. Toss well. Set the vegetables aside for 15 minutes to allow them to absorb the dressing.

- Arrange the lettuce leaves on a serving platter.

- Place the marinated potatoes, green beans, and tomatoes in the center of the lettuce.

- Drain the tuna, flake it with a fork, and place it around the potatoes. Drizzle the remaining dressing over the salad.

- Cut the eggs into quarters and set the eggs and olives around the edge of the platter.

- Serve accompanied with French bread for a complete summer meal.

Chef's Tip

You may remove the pits from the Niçoise olives before serving them, but it will be easier to simply remind your guests that the olives have pits and to nibble around them.

Tossed Salad with Cheese Croutons
Salade des Moines

The Burgundy region of France produces some of the most famous cow's milk cheeses in the country. The salad dressing for this dish uses the popular local walnut oil, and Dijon mustard. The recipe also calls for *port salut* cheese melted on slices of French bread or baguettes and served alongside the salad. Port salut is available in most supermarkets or specialty cheese stores. It has a creamy, mild flavor that you will really like.

Serves 4

Ingredients

1 head of Boston bibb or butter lettuce

1 tablespoon sherry vinegar

2 tablespoons walnut oil

½ teaspoon Dijon mustard

¼ teaspoon salt

freshly ground black pepper

1 loaf French baguette (recipe page 34)

8 ounces *port salut* or Gruyère cheese

On your mark, get set . . .

- Fill a clean sink with fresh cold water.

- Separate the leaves of the lettuce and drop them into the water. Let them soak for a few minutes, gently moving them around with your hands to help dislodge any dirt.

- Remove the leaves and place them in a colander. Drain the water from the sink and clean any dirt or sand from the bottom.

- Refill the sink and repeat the washing at least once.

- Use a salad spinner to dry the greens. If you don't have a spinner, lay paper toweling on a clean countertop and place the greens on it. Gently roll up the leaves in the paper towels to absorb the extra moisture. You may have to do this in two batches. Tear the lettuce into small pieces and set aside.

- Pour the vinegar, oil, Dijon mustard, salt, and pepper into the bottom of a large salad bowl. Whisk together to combine.

- Add the lettuce to the bowl with the dressing. Toss the salad in the dressing being careful to get the dressing equally distributed on the lettuce.

- Divide the tossed salad between four plates and set aside while you make the croutons.

Cook!

- Place an oven rack in the top slot of the oven. Ask your adult assistant to preheat the broiler to high. Cut the baguette into 12 slices and lay them on a baking tray. Cut the cheese into thin slices and top each piece of bread with 1 slice of cheese.

- Place the tray under the broiler for 30 to 45 seconds or until the cheese melts and just begins to brown.

- Lay 3 croutons on each plate and serve immediately.

French Bread
Pain Baguette

What French meal would be complete without a crusty, crisp loaf of home-made bread? France is home to some of the best breads in the world. Making good bread requires patience and some simple planning. The rewards, however, of the aroma of fresh bread baking and the taste of your homemade bread will easily make up for the time spent preparing it.

Serves 6

Ingredients

1 cup warm water (100°F-110°F)

1 package (¼ ounce) active dry yeast

1 tablespoon sugar

3 ½ cups unbleached all-purpose flour

1 ½ teaspoons salt

1 tablespoon ground cornmeal

On your mark . . .

- Pour the cup of warm water into a small bowl. Make sure the water is not too hot, which will stop the yeast from becoming active, or too cool, which will keep it from starting. Run the water over your fingers for a few seconds to make sure it is just warm.

- Sprinkle the package of yeast over the water, add the sugar, and give it a stir.

- Cover it and let it stand for 5 minutes. You will know the yeast is active if after 5 minutes, soft bubbles appear on the surface of the water. If the bubbles do not appear, it means the yeast did not become active. Simply discard it and repeat this step with a new package of yeast and fresh warm water.

Get set . . .

- Place 3 cups of the flour in a large bowl. Sprinkle on the salt.

- Make a well in the center. Pour the yeast mixture into the well. Combine the yeast mixture and flour with a fork until it forms a soft, loose dough.

- Sprinkle 1 tablespoon of the remaining flour on a clean work surface. Empty the dough out of the bowl, making sure to get any extra flour that remains in the bottom.

- Sprinkle a little flour on your hands and begin kneading the dough by pressing it away from you with the palms of your hands and then folding it in half. Pick it up and give it a turn to the right or left. Sprinkle extra water on the dough if it is too dry, or add a little extra flour if it is too wet.

- Continue to knead the dough for 5 to 6 minutes. Remember to keep turning it in the same direction. The dough will be sticky in the beginning, but don't worry. Every so often, give the dough a few punches to get the air out. Knead it until it's smooth and springy.

- The dough is now ready for a rest. Place it in a large clean bowl. Cover it with a clean, lightly floured kitchen towel. Lay another clean towel on top and place the dough in a warm, draft-free spot to rise undisturbed for 1 ½ hours, or until doubled in size.

- Return the dough to a lightly floured work surface and punch it flat to force out the air. Knead the dough for another 4 to 5 minutes.

- Place the dough in a clean bowl, cover again with the lightly floured towel, and let it rise undisturbed for 1 hour, or until it has doubled in size.

Cook!

- Preheat the oven to 425°F.

- After the dough has risen twice, it will be ready to shape into long loaves. To make 2 baguettes: Lightly flour the work surface. Pull the dough out of the bowl. Cut it in half and cover one half with the floured towel, while you shape the other half.

- Flatten the dough and press out the air. Check to see if the dough is sticking to your work surface. If so, gently lift it and sprinkle a bit of flour underneath.

- Press and shape the dough into a long rectangle.

- Create a line down the middle with the side of your hand, karate-chop-style, and then fold it in half lengthwise. Pinch the dough closed along the two edges and then pinch the ends of the dough together.

- Sprinkle the cornmeal on a lightly greased baking sheet and gently lift the dough onto the baking sheet. If necessary, shape its length to fit the baking sheet. Cover with the floured towel.

- Repeat these steps with the other half of the dough.

- Use a sharp knife and make a few diagonal cuts across the surface of the loaves to allow the bread to expand as it bakes. Place the baguettes in the oven and bake for 35 to 40 minutes, or until the loaves are browned and crisp.

- Remove the baguettes to a rack and let cool.

Ham and Cheese Crunches
Croque-Monsieur

The cafés and bistros in Paris are busy at lunchtime with large numbers of local diners and tourists. Smart Parisians know the right places to find appealing sandwiches. First served in 1910 at a Parisian café, this version of a ham and cheese sandwich is still popular today. The name *croque-monsieur* literally means "crunch-sir." Try this popular version of a bistro recipe and you will say, *"Vive la France!"*

Serves 4

Ingredients

8 slices thin sandwich bread

4 slices smoked or boiled ham (1 ounce each)

4 ounces Gruyère or Swiss cheese

3 tablespoons milk

3 tablespoons melted butter

On your mark, get set . . .

- Preheat the oven to 400°F.

- Cut away the crusts of the bread with a sharp knife. Discard the crusts. Lay 4 of the slices on a small baking sheet.

- Cut the ham so it neatly fits the slices of bread, with none extending over the sides. You will probably have more than one layer of ham, but that is okay.

- Grate the Gruyère or Swiss cheese into a small bowl. Add the milk and combine with the cheese.

- Spoon one-quarter of the cheese mixture on top of the ham on one sandwich, and cover with a slice of bread.

- With a pastry brush, butter the top slice. Carefully turn the sandwich over and butter the bottom slice.

- Repeat these steps to assemble the other 3 crunches.

Cook!

- Place the baking sheet in the oven and bake the sandwiches for 10 to 15 minutes, or until the cheese melts and the bread just begins to brown.

- Turn the oven to broil. Brown the sandwiches under the broiler for 1 minute on each side. If necessary, reshape the sandwiches with a spatula after you turn them, tapping in the sides like a deck of cards. Be careful not to let them burn.

- Lift the finished crunches off the baking sheet with a spatula to a serving dish. Let cool for a moment, cut into quarters, and serve hot.

Cheese soufflé.

Cheese Soufflé
Soufflé au Fromage

Making a soufflé will prove to you that there is real magic in French cooking. What is a soufflé? It is a flavored sauce into which fluffy egg whites are carefully folded. The beaten egg whites lighten the sauce with air and allow it to puff up while it bakes to a golden brown. Most people think it is difficult to make a soufflé successfully. Not true! The recipe works if you follow its few basic steps and use very fresh eggs. The best part of making a soufflé is watching the excited faces of your guests as you carry your golden creation to the table.

Serves 6

Ingredients

FOR THE MOLD

1 tablespoon butter

2 ½ tablespoons grated Parmesan cheese

FOR THE SOUFFLÉ

1 cup whole milk

3 tablespoons butter

3 tablespoons all-purpose flour

½ teaspoon salt

¼ teaspoon paprika

pinch ground black or cayenne pepper

1 cup grated Swiss cheese, or ½ cup grated Swiss cheese and ½ cup grated Parmesan cheese combined

5 eggs

On your mark, get set . . .

- Butter the insides of a 6-cup soufflé mold or round baking dish, making sure to evenly cover the bottom as well as the sides.

- Sprinkle the grated Parmesan into the mold. Roll and tip the mold back and forth until all the surfaces are lightly covered with the cheese. Tap out any excess cheese. Refrigerate the mold.

- Measure the milk, butter, flour, salt, paprika, and pepper and set aside.

- Grate the Swiss cheese, using the largest holes of the grater, and set aside.

- To separate the eggs, you will need three bowls: two small bowls (one to hold the egg yolks and one to hold the whites) and one large nonaluminum bowl to beat the egg whites in.

- Holding an egg in one hand, break the shell in two with a firm tap on the edge of one of the small bowls. Pour the egg yolk back and forth between the two shells, allowing the egg white to fall away from the shell into the small bowl below. Once most of the egg white is separated, pour the yolk into the other small bowl. Make sure there is no egg yolk in the egg whites, or they will not whip properly.

- Continue with the remaining eggs, following the same steps, until all the eggs are separated.

Cook!

- Preheat the oven to 400°F.

- In a 1-quart saucepan, heat the milk on medium-low heat, but don't let it boil.

- In the meantime, melt the butter in a 2 ½-quart saucepan on medium-low heat. When the butter has melted and has begun to bubble, add the flour.

- Mix the butter and flour together with a wooden spoon or whisk, and continue stirring for 1 to 2 minutes over the heat. Be careful not to let the flour and butter brown. If that starts to happen, lift the pan and reduce the heat.

- Remove the pan from the heat and add the hot milk all at once. Stir it until you have a smooth sauce.

- Add the egg yolks, one at a time, whisking each in completely before adding the next. After all the egg yolks have been stirred into the sauce, mix in the salt, paprika, and pepper, then set aside.

Pour the egg whites into the larger bowl and, with an electric hand mixer, beat them on low speed for 1 minute, then gradually raise the speed to high. Move the beaters back and forth and rotate the bowl as the egg whites start to stiffen. This will take 3 to 4 minutes. Turn off the mixer.

Scoop a large spoonful of the whites out of the bowl. If they are firm and hold their shape in stiff peaks, they are ready for the sauce. If not, beat them for another 1 or 2 minutes.

Add one-quarter of the beaten whites on top of the sauce and gently stir them in.

Scoop the rest of the beaten whites on top of the sauce and sprinkle on one-quarter of the grated cheese.

Start folding the mixture together with a rubber spatula. Folding means that instead of blending the egg whites with a spoon in a circular motion, you blend with a spatula in an up and down, or under and over, motion. Give the bowl a quarter turn and repeat this step until you have lightly folded the whites into the sauce and all the cheese has been added. Some of the whites should not completely blend into the sauce, so don't overmix it.

Pour the soufflé mixture into the mold and smooth the top of the soufflé with the spatula to make it even.

The soufflé is now ready to bake. Place it in the lower third of the oven and close the door. Immediately turn down the oven to 375°F. Bake the soufflé for 30 to 35 minutes, or until puffy and golden brown. Don't be tempted to open the oven door while it is baking—the soufflé may fall.

Carry the soufflé to the table and serve at once. Hold a serving spoon and fork back-to-back over the center of the soufflé. Sink them into the center and pull the soufflé apart into serving portions.

Bacon and Egg Custard Tart
Quiche Lorraine

This classic recipe from the region of Alsace-Lorraine dates back to the sixteenth century when, so they say, quiche Lorraine was created to celebrate the coming of spring and served on May Day. It is simple to make, beautiful to look at, and delicious. That is probably why it has been a favorite for centuries. Try making your own pie crust (page 48) for the shell, or buy a frozen one. Just check the frozen pie shell package and pick one with natural ingredients. This is a rich recipe, so you probably won't want to eat it every day, but it is a great dish for a special occasion.

Serves 6

Ingredients

flour for rolling out pastry

1 recipe pie crust (page 48) or 1 frozen 9-inch pie shell

6 slices thick-cut smoked bacon (4 ounces, or ¾ cup chopped)

4 eggs

1 ½ cups heavy cream, or 1 cup whole milk and ½ cup heavy cream combined

freshly ground black pepper to taste

On your mark, get set . . .

- Preheat the oven to 375°F.

- If using your own pie shell: Lightly flour a clean work surface. Sprinkle a little flour on a rolling pin and roll it back and forth a few times to completely cover it with flour. Lay the chilled pastry on the work surface and sprinkle the top lightly with flour.

- Lay the rolling pin in the center of the pastry and gently but firmly roll the pin back and forth to flatten it. Now start rolling out the pastry, always starting from the center and rolling just to the edges of the pastry. Pick the pastry up and give it a slight turn. Repeat these steps until the pastry is about ⅛ inch thick and a few inches larger than a 9-inch pie dish.

- Place the rolling pin on top of the farthest edge of the pastry. Bring the edge up and over the rolling pin. Roll the rest of the pastry onto the rolling pin. Lift the rolling pin and place it over the center of the pie dish.

- Unroll the pastry and let it sink into the shape of the dish. Try not to stretch it. Leave at least 1 inch of pastry overhanging the edge, then cut away the excess pastry.

- To make a decorative edge, roll over the edge of the pastry and gently press your finger into it to give it a slightly curved shape. Repeat this all around the edge.

- Chill the shell while you prepare the other ingredients.

- If using a frozen pie shell: Follow the package directions for the best results.

Cook!

- Cut the bacon into small strips about 1 inch wide and ¼ inch thick.

- Cook the bacon in a 10-inch skillet on medium heat until it starts to turn brown and slightly crisp. Drain the bacon on paper towels and set aside.

- Beat together the eggs and cream, or milk and cream combination, with a whisk or electric hand mixer until frothy. This is called the custard. Add the pepper.

- Remove the pie shell from the refrigerator and place it on a baking sheet.

- Press the bacon pieces gently into the bottom of the shell.

- Pour the custard over the top, being careful not to fill the shell more than three-quarters full.

- Place the quiche on the middle rack of the oven and bake for 30 to 35 minutes. The quiche will puff up and turn golden brown.

- Let it rest for 10 minutes before slicing and serving.

Pie Crust *Pate Brisee*

In France the making of pastry is truly an art and a labor of love. This recipe can be used for the quiche Lorraine recipe on page 46 or if you just need a perfect pastry crust recipe for pies. You can make the crust by hand, or in a food processor. Ask your adult assistant to help you if you are making it in the food processor.

Makes 1 9-inch pie shell

Ingredients

1 ¼ cups unbleached all-purpose flour

¼ teaspoon salt

4 tablespoons frozen unsalted butter

1 ½ tablespoons vegetable oil

2 ½ to 3 tablespoons ice water

On your mark, get set, chill!
To make in a food processor:
- Ask your adult assistant to carefully insert the all-purpose blade in the bowl of the food processor.

- Add the flour and salt and lock the lid into place.

- Pulse the mixture on and off 6 times.

- Cut the frozen butter into chunks. Remove the lid and add the butter and the oil to the flour.

- Process for 15 seconds as you slowly pour in the ice water, 1 tablespoon at a time. Continue to add the ice water until the dough just comes together into a ball.

- Turn off the processor. If the dough is too wet you may add a teaspoon or more flour. Process until the dough comes together. If the dough is too loose you can add a few teaspoons more ice water and process until the dough comes together into a ball.

- Ask your adult assistant to carefully remove the dough.

- Dust the ball of dough with a little flour. Wrap the pastry dough in wax paper or plastic wrap and refrigerate for at least 1 hour or overnight.

To make by hand:
- Sift the flour and salt together into a large bowl.

- Cut the butter into small chunks and add to the bowl.

- Using a pastry cutter, or the tips of your fingers, blend the mixture until it comes together into crumbs the size of small peas. Pour 1 tablespoon of ice water on the dough and blend together using a fork. Add another tablespoon of the ice water and continue to mix with the fork until the dough is no longer loose.

- Sprinkle a little flour on a clean countertop, or cutting board, and pull the dough from the bowl. Shape the dough into a ball and dust it with a little flour, wrap in wax paper or plastic wrap and refrigerate for at least 1 hour or overnight.

Cheese Puffs *Gougéres*

In Burgundy these delicate cheese puffs are the perfect way to start a meal. This is the same basic recipe that is used to make cream puffs recipe (page 84), but here Parmesan cheese is added to make this savory delight. Parmesan cheese should always be grated fresh to achieve the best flavor.

Makes 12 cheese puffs

Ingredients

1 stick unsalted butter (8 tablespoons) plus 1 ½ teaspoons for baking tray

1 cup all-purpose flour plus a little extra for dusting

½ teaspoon salt

1 cup water

4 large eggs (not extra-large or jumbo)

1 ½ cups grated Parmesan cheese

On your mark, get set . . .

- Preheat the oven to 400°F.

- Lightly butter a large baking sheet with 1 ½ teaspoons of the butter and dust with a tablespoon or so of the flour.

- Shake the baking sheet back and forth until the entire surface is coated with flour.

- Avoid touching the coated surface. Turn the sheet over and tap out the excess flour. Set the baking sheet aside.

- Measure 1 cup flour and ½ teaspoon salt and set aside.

Cook!

- Add the water, 1 stick butter, and salt to a medium-size saucepan, and place on low heat.

- Bring to a soft boil and cook until the butter has melted.

- Remove the pan from the heat, add the flour all at once, and stir very well with a wooden spoon for about a minute to make sure all the flour is mixed in.

- Place the pan back on the stove and turn the heat to medium.

Continue to cook and stir for another 2 minutes. You will see a light film form on the bottom of the pan as you stir. Remove the pan from the heat.

- Pour the dough into a large bowl. Let it cool for about a minute.

- Add 1 egg and beat it into the mixture with an electric hand mixer on low speed. When it is completely mixed in, add another egg and mix in.

- Continue with the third egg and then the fourth. The last egg that is added should bring the dough together into a shiny yellow dough. Add the cheese and beat it into the dough.

- To make the cheese puffs: Use two tablespoons, one to scoop the dough and one to push the dough off onto the baking sheet in 12 rounded spoonfuls.

- Space the spoonfuls of dough about 3 inches apart. Give the tops a little tap to help round them.

- Bake for 25 to 30 minutes, or until puffed and golden.

- Serve the puffs warm or at room temperature.

Roast chicken and glazed carrots.

Scallops in Cream Sauce
Coquilles St. Jacques

Scallops from the waters of the Atlantic are prepared in regional recipes throughout France. This dish, however, is a true favorite. When you try this recipe, you will learn to make a simple cream sauce. You will also learn to make a thickening agent called a roux, one of the most important steps in creating rich sauces in French cooking.

Serves 6

Ingredients

1 pound fresh or fully thawed frozen scallops

1 ½ tablespoons chopped shallot or green onion

1 tablespoon chopped fresh flat-leaf parsley

1 bay leaf

¼ teaspoon dried thyme

6 ounces fresh mushrooms

2 tablespoons butter

2 tablespoons all-purpose flour

⅓ cup heavy cream

1 cup whole milk

salt and freshly ground black pepper to taste

On your mark, get set . . .

- Rinse the scallops under cold running water and drain well.

- If the scallops are large, slice them in half and set aside. If they are small or you are using bay scallops, leave them whole.

- Peel and chop the shallot or green onion and measure 1 ½ tablespoons.

- Chop the parsley.

- On a small plate, place the parsley, shallot, bay leaf, and dried thyme, and set aside.

- Clean the mushrooms with a dry paper towel and thinly slice them. Measure 2 cups and set aside.

- Measure the butter and flour and set aside.

Cook!

- To prepare the sauce: Start by making a thickening agent called a roux. In a small saucepan, melt the butter on low heat. Add the flour and blend them together until smooth. Cook the roux slowly for 2 minutes—the butter and flour will gently bubble.

- Add the cream and ½ cup of the milk. Mix with a whisk until you have a smooth sauce.

- Simmer the sauce for 3 to 4 minutes, stirring occasionally to keep it from sticking. Be careful the sauce doesn't brown; reduce the heat if it does. The sauce will be thick, but you will thin it later. Remove it from the stove and set aside.

- Next make the poaching liquid for the scallops: Pour the remaining ½ cup milk into a 4-quart saucepan. Add the shallot, bay leaf, thyme, parsley, salt, and pepper, and bring to a soft simmer on medium-low heat. Cook for 3 minutes.

- Add the scallops, cover the pan, and cook on low heat for 3 minutes. The scallops should feel a little springy when you touch them and change in color from pink to almost white.

- Remove the scallops from the pan with a slotted spoon to a warm bowl and set aside. Remove the bay leaf from the poaching liquid and discard.

- Increase the heat to medium, add the sliced mushrooms, and bring to a boil. Cook for 3 to 4 minutes, or until the mushrooms are tender.

- Add the cream sauce to the pan with the mushrooms and blend all the ingredients into a smooth sauce.

- Return the scallops to the sauce and simmer for another 1 or 2 minutes. Serve hot.

Turbot with Fresh Vegetables
Gigot de Palavas

From the province of Languedoc on the Mediterranean coast comes this recipe for fresh turbot. The technique used here of enriching flavor with thin slices of garlic is one that dates back hundreds of years in French cooking. Use only a boneless fillet of fresh fish that is in one piece and you will get the best results.

Serves 6

Ingredients

1 ½ pounds fresh turbot, cod, haddock, salmon, red snapper, or monkfish, in one piece

1 medium-size onion (1 cup chopped)

1 medium-size red or green bell pepper

1 or 2 fresh tomatoes (about 1 pound)

2 medium-size zucchini

1 small eggplant

3 cloves garlic

¼ cup extra-virgin olive oil

2 teaspoons salt for seasoning

¼ teaspoon freshly ground black pepper

On your mark . . .

- Rinse and pat dry the fillet of fish.

- Run your clean hands across the surface of the fish, and check for any bones that might be poking through. If you find any, remove them by using a clean piece of paper towel to grip the tip of the bone and pull it out. Cover and refrigerate the fish.

- Peel and chop the onion. Measure 1 cup and set aside.

- Wash the rest of the vegetables. Cut the pepper in half and remove the stem and seeds. Cut each half into long thin strips and set aside.

- Remove the stem ends from the tomatoes. Chop the tomatoes into chunks, measure 1 to 1 ½ cups, and set aside.

- Cut the zucchini into chunks, measure 2 cups, and set aside.
- Cut the eggplant into cubes, measure 2 cups, and set aside.
- Peel and chop 1 clove of the garlic and set aside.

Get set . . .

- Remove the fish from the refrigerator and lay it on a clean cutting board.
- Slightly crush the remaining 2 cloves of garlic with the flat side of a knife and remove the skin. Slice the garlic cloves into very thin slivers.
- With the tip of your knife, make several small slits in the surface of the fish fillet. Insert a sliver of garlic into one of the slits and gently push the garlic into the fish. Repeat until all the slivers have been used and the surface of the fish is dotted with garlic.
- Cover the fish with plastic wrap and return it to the refrigerator. Wash the cutting board and put it away.

Cook!

- In an ovenproof baking dish with a lid, heat the olive oil on low heat on the stove. Add the chopped onion and sauté for about 4 minutes, or until golden in color.
- Add the red or green pepper strips and cook for about 2 minutes, or until slightly tender.
- Add the chopped garlic, zucchini, eggplant, tomatoes, salt, and pepper. Give the vegetables a few stirs to combine, then let them cook slowly for 20 minutes uncovered. Add a little water if the vegetables begin to dry out or stick to the bottom as they are cooking.
- Preheat the oven to 350°F.
- After 20 minutes, remove the fish from the refrigerator and lay it on top of the vegetables. Spoon some of the sauce from the vegetables over the fish.
- Cover the baking dish and place in the oven. Bake for 25 minutes. About halfway through the baking, lift the lid and baste the

fish with more of the sauce. The fish is done when it flakes and separates. Serve hot.

Chef's Tip

For a perfect summer supper, make this dish ahead of time, let it chill, and serve it cold.

Roast Chicken
Poulet Rôti Entier

The French are masters at many things in the kitchen, and roast chicken is unquestionably one of them. Baking a chicken to a golden brown with crispy skin is not difficult. The first thing to remember is that the freshest chicken makes the best roast chicken. If possible, look for organic, free-range chickens. Follow the steps to prepare the chicken carefully before it goes in the oven, along with a few simple food safety tips, and you're guaranteed a great-tasting chicken.

Serves 4

Ingredients

1 whole chicken, preferably organic/free-range
   (3 ½ to 4 pounds)

salt and freshly ground black pepper to taste

cotton string or butcher's cord

1 tablespoon butter or olive oil

1 carrot

1 stalk celery

1 onion

1 cup homemade chicken stock (page 22)
   or canned low-sodium chicken broth

1 tablespoon butter

On your mark, get set . . .

- Preheat the oven to 450°F.

- Remove all the packing material the chicken is wrapped in and discard it. Inside the chicken you will probably find a package of chicken parts. Remove and save the parts for chicken stock, or discard them. Trim any excess fat from the chicken and discard.

- Rinse the chicken under cold running water and pat dry with a paper towel, inside and out; a dry chicken will roast to a perfect golden brown. Season the inside of the chicken with a little salt and pepper.

- With a 36-inch length of cotton string or butcher's cord, tie the end of one leg on top of the other so they are crossed over and together. Fold the wings under in a "laid-back" fashion by taking the tip of each wing and folding it under itself. Pull the string under the chicken and wrap the wings together by pulling the string across the top of the wings. Pull snugly to make a tight bundle and tie the ends together to keep the string secure.

- Place the chicken, breast side up, on a rack inside a lightly oiled roasting pan. The pan should be about 2 inches deep and just large enough to hold the chicken.

- Rub 1 tablespoon butter or oil all over the skin of the chicken and season with salt and pepper. Wash your hands and all work surfaces with hot soapy water.

- Wash and chop the carrot and celery. Peel the onion, chop in large pieces, and set aside.

Cook!

- Place the roasting pan with the chicken on the lower middle rack of the oven. Set the timer for 25 minutes and bake the chicken without peeking.

- When the timer rings, reduce the heat to 350°F. Open the oven door and, using a large spoon, baste the chicken with the juices from the bottom of the pan. Ask an adult for assistance in basting.

- Scatter the chopped vegetables around the pan, close the oven door, and continue to bake. Set the timer for 40 minutes and when it rings, baste again.

- Set the timer for another 40 minutes and baste a final time. Total cooking time is 1 hour 45 minutes, or until a meat thermometer inserted in the thigh reaches 180°F.

- Prick the skin of the lower thigh with a fork. The juices that run from it should be clear, with no trace of pink color. If pink, let the chicken cook for another 5 to 10 minutes.

- Remove the chicken from the oven to a warm platter and let it rest for 20 minutes.

- Ask your adult assistant to remove the string and carve the chicken as you prepare the sauce from the pan drippings. To do this, tip the roasting pan slightly and remove and discard all but

1 tablespoon of the fat. Leave the cooked vegetables in the pan for added flavor.

- Place the roasting pan on medium heat on the stove and add the chicken stock. Bring it to a boil. Carefully scrape up any stuck bits from the bottom of the pan with a large spoon. Watch that the sauce does not burn.

- Continue to boil as you add the remaining 1 tablespoon butter and the sauce reduces. Boil for 6 or 8 minutes as the sauce thickens, then reduce the heat and simmer for 3 to 4 minutes, or until slightly thickened.

- Place the carved chicken pieces on a serving platter and pass the sauce at the table.

Chef's Tip

Use only cord that is made of natural fibers; otherwise it will melt in the oven and the chicken will have to be discarded.

Chicken with Apples and Cream
Poulet Vallée d'Auge

The apples of Normandy are legendary. Apple harvest time in this ancient land is a reason for celebration. Try this adaptation of a regional recipe and you'll understand why the modest apple has such a place of honor in French cooking.

Serves 6

Ingredients

1 chicken, cut into 8 pieces, preferably organic/free-range (3 ½ pounds)

½ teaspoon salt

⅛ teaspoon freshly ground black pepper

3 tablespoons butter

1 tablespoon extra-virgin olive oil

2 ½ tablespoons apple cider vinegar

½ teaspoon sugar

2 tablespoons chopped shallots or green onions

2 golden delicious apples (about 1 ½ cups chopped)

½ cup plus 1 tablespoon apple cider

¼ cup heavy cream

On your mark, get set . . .

- Rinse the chicken pieces under cold running water and pat dry with a paper towel. Make sure to dry the chicken thoroughly, or it will spatter when it is browned. Season the chicken with the salt and pepper and refrigerate until ready to use.

- Measure the butter, olive oil, apple cider vinegar, and sugar.

- Peel and chop the shallots or green onions into small pieces.

- Cut the apples in half and then into quarters. Remove the stems and the cores, using a small sharp knife.

- Cut the quarters into small chunks and drop them into a bowl with 1 tablespoon of the apple cider. Toss the cut apples in the cider; this will keep them from turning brown.

- Put the chicken, butter, olive oil, vinegar, sugar, shallots, and apples close by the stove.

Cook!

- Heat 2 tablespoons of the butter and 1 tablespoon olive oil in a 12-inch skillet on low heat.

- Place the chicken pieces in the skillet, a few at a time, and brown on all sides. Remove the browned pieces to a clean platter and continue cooking until all the chicken is brown.

- Ask an adult assistant to help you drain the fat from the skillet. Return the skillet to medium heat.

- Add the remaining 1 tablespoon butter along with the chopped shallots, apples, sugar, and apple cider vinegar. Raise the heat to medium and cook for 2 to 3 minutes, gently scraping the bottom of the pan to loosen all the brown bits.

- Return the chicken pieces to the skillet along with any juices that are in the bottom of the platter.

- Add the remaining ½ cup apple cider and the cream. Baste all the pieces of chicken with the sauce.

- Reduce the heat to simmer. Cook uncovered for 35 to 40 minutes, or until the chicken is cooked through to the bone and tender.

- Remove the chicken pieces to a clean serving platter, cover loosely with foil, and keep warm.

- Place a large hand strainer over a saucepan. Pour the ingredients from the skillet into the strainer and, with the back of a wooden spoon, press down on the apples and push the juices into the pan. Discard what is left in the strainer.

- Bring the sauce to a boil on medium-high heat. Boil the sauce until it reduces by half.

- Return the chicken to the skillet and add the reduced sauce. Cook for about 2 to 3 minutes, or until the chicken is heated through.

- Place the chicken pieces on the serving platter, top with the sauce, and take piping hot to the table.

Roast Pork with Dried Plums

Longe de Porc aux Pruneaux

This recipe comes from the heartland of France, the Loire Valley region. The richness of roasted pork and the subtle sweetness of the dried fruits make it perfect for a special occasion or holiday dinner. Why wait till then? Try it now and see how it will make any dinner a special occasion.

Ingredients

½ cup dried pitted plums

½ cup dark raisins

1 teaspoon sugar

1 cup hot water

1 small onion

1 carrot

2 tablespoons butter

1 boneless pork loin roast (2 ½ pounds)

1 tablespoon balsamic vinegar

½ teaspoon dried thyme

½ teaspoon salt

¼ teaspoon freshly ground black pepper

½ cup homemade chicken stock (page 22) or canned low-sodium chicken broth

3 tablespoons heavy cream

On your mark, get set . . .

- Check the dried plums for pits and place the pitted plums in a small bowl.

- Add the raisins, sprinkle on the sugar, and add the hot water. Let the dried fruits soak for at least 30 minutes.

- Peel and chop the onion and measure ½ cup.

- Wash and chop the carrot and measure ½ cup.

Cook!

- Preheat the oven to 375°F.

- In a roasting pan large enough to hold all the ingredients, melt the butter on medium-low heat.

- When the butter begins to bubble, add the roast and turn it to brown on all sides. A sturdy pair of tongs works great for this. After the roast has browned, remove it to a clean plate.

- Add the onion, carrot, and balsamic vinegar to the roasting pan and cook for 2 to 3 minutes.

- Return the roast to the pan on top of the vegetables. Add the dried fruit mixture with the soaking liquid, thyme, salt, and pepper.

- Place the roasting pan on the middle rack of the oven and roast the pork uncovered for 1 ½ hours. Every ½ hour, baste the roast with the liquid in the bottom of the pan.

- After 1 ½ hours, the roast should be very tender and a meat thermometer placed in the center of the roast should read 165°F to 170°F. Remove the pork to a warm serving platter and loosely cover with foil.

- Place the roasting pan on the stovetop on medium-low heat and add the chicken stock. Bring to a simmer and cook for 2 to 4 minutes, skimming off and discarding any fat on the surface.

- Add the cream and cook for 2 to 3 minutes, but do not boil.

- Slice the roast into serving pieces and place on the platter, surrounded with the vegetables and fruit.

- Pour the finished sauce from the roasting pan into a separate serving bowl and pass it at the table.

Beef Stew with Tomatoes and Olives

Daube de Boeuf à la Provençale

Before ovens were common in French kitchens, cooking was done over open fires. Iron pots with lids hollowed out to hold hot coals slowly cooked many meals with wonderfully flavorful results. Slow-cooking, or braising, beef in a broth enhanced with vegetables creates the French stews that are some of the best in the world. Every region of France has its own version of this dish, but this recipe is an adaptation of a classic from Provence.

Serves 6

Ingredients

FOR THE BEEF

1 medium-size onion

1 clove garlic

2 carrots

3 medium-size ripe tomatoes (about 1 pound)

2 tablespoons red wine vinegar

1 cup Niçoise or pitted black olives

½ pound mushrooms

2 ½ pounds top round or sirloin beef, cut into 1 ½-inch cubes

1 teaspoon salt

¼ teaspoon dried thyme

FOR THE POT

½ pound thick-cut smoked bacon

3 tablespoons all-purpose flour

¾ cup homemade chicken stock (page 22) or canned low-sodium chicken broth

2 to 3 tablespoons chopped fresh flat-leaf parsley for garnish

On your mark, get set . . .

- To prepare the beef: Peel and chop the onion into medium-size chunks and measure 1 cup.

- Peel, crush, and chop the garlic.

- Wash and chop the carrots and measure 1 cup.

- Wash the tomatoes and remove the stem ends. Cut the tomatoes into small chunks and measure 2 ½ to 3 cups.

- Measure the vinegar and 1 cup drained pitted olives.

- Clean the mushrooms with a dry paper towel and cut into quarters.

- Place all the ingredients for the beef in a nonaluminum bowl large enough to hold everything, and mix well. Set the beef and vegetables aside to marinate.

- Cut the bacon into 3-inch pieces.

- Measure the flour and chicken stock and set aside.

Cook!

- Bring 1 cup water to a boil in a small saucepan on medium-high heat. Add the bacon pieces, reduce the heat to low, and simmer for 3 to 4 minutes. Drain the bacon and set aside.

- Place an ovenproof pot, with a lid, large enough to hold all the ingredients on the stove. Lay one-third of the bacon pieces on the bottom of the pot.

- With a slotted spoon, add about one-third of the marinated beef and vegetables on top of the bacon.

- Sprinkle on 1 tablespoon of the flour.

- Layer on another third of the bacon, then another third of the beef and vegetables, and top with 1 tablespoon flour.

- Make the last layer with the remaining bacon, then the beef, and top with the remaining 1 tablespoon flour.

- Pour any liquid left from the marinade over the top and add the chicken stock.

- Turn the heat to medium and bring the pot to a simmer. This will take about 10 minutes.

- Reduce the heat to low, cover the pan with the lid slightly ajar, and cook for 30 minutes, keeping the pot cooking at a gentle boil. If it is cooking too fast, reduce the heat.

- Preheat the oven to 350°F.

- After 30 minutes, remove the lid, cover the pot with a sheet of aluminum foil, and then replace the lid. Place the pot on the middle rack of the oven and bake for 1 hour 30 minutes.

- Serve hot, sprinkled with the chopped parsley.

Chef's Tip

This dish can be served over buttered egg noodles, prepared according to the package directions. If using Niçoise olives, remove the pits by gently crushing the olives with the flat side of a large knife. Discard the pits.

Vegetable Casserole
Ratatouille

Ratatouille is the ultimate vegetable dish and it comes from Provence. Don't be discouraged that it takes a little extra time to prepare. The final results are worth the effort. Ratatouille is going to make you feel very differently about eating your vegetables!

Serves 6

Ingredients

1 medium-size eggplant

3 medium-size zucchini

2 ½ teaspoons salt

1 red onion

2 red bell peppers

1 clove garlic

3 medium-size ripe tomatoes (about 1 ½ to 2 pounds)

3 tablespoons chopped fresh flat-leaf parsley

5 tablespoons extra-virgin olive oil

freshly ground black pepper to taste

On your mark . . .

- Wash and peel the eggplant. Cut the eggplant into ½-inch slices, then cut each slice into quarters and measure about 3 cups.

- Wash the zucchini very well to remove any sand, then cut into ½-inch slices and measure about 4 cups.

- To remove excess moisture and bitter juices from the eggplant and zucchini, place them in two separate nonaluminum bowls and toss each with 1 teaspoon of the salt. Set aside for 20 to 30 minutes.

Get set . . .

- Peel and thinly slice the onion.

- Wash the peppers and cut in half. Remove the stems and seeds. Cut the halves into thin strips.

- Peel, crush, and chop the garlic.

- Wash the tomatoes and remove the stem ends. Chop the tomatoes into chunks and measure about 3 cups.

- Chop the parsley and set aside.

- Drain the eggplant and zucchini. To dry, lay a couple of sheets of paper towels on a tray or on the counter. Place the drained eggplant, a handful at a time, on the paper towels. Lay another sheet of paper towels over them and gently pat dry. Place the dried pieces in a bowl and repeat this step until all the eggplant and zucchini are dry.

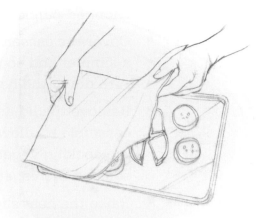

Cook!

- Place a 2 ½-quart heatproof casserole or heavy-bottomed pot, with a lid, next to the stove.

- Heat a 10- to 12-inch skillet with 1 tablespoon of the olive oil on medium heat.

- Sauté the zucchini slices for about 1 to 2 minutes on each side, until just beginning to brown. Remove them to a clean plate.

- Add 2 tablespoons of the olive oil to the skillet and sauté the eggplant, lightly browning on both sides, and place it on a clean plate.

- Add the remaining 2 tablespoons olive oil to the skillet and sauté the onion and peppers for 10 minutes, or until they are soft.

- Add the tomatoes, garlic, remaining ½ teaspoon salt, and pepper. Cook for 5 to 7 minutes, or until the tomatoes start to release their liquid. Turn off the heat.

- Spoon about one-third of the tomato mixture into the bottom of the casserole. Top with one-third of the eggplant and one-third of the zucchini, then sprinkle on 1 tablespoon of the parsley.

- Make another layer with one-third more of the tomato mixture, one-third of the eggplant and zucchini, and 1 tablespoon of the parsley.

- Make the last layer with the remaining vegetables, following the same layering steps, and sprinkle with the remaining 1 tablespoon chopped parsley.

- Cover the casserole and place it on low heat. Bring the stew to a simmer and cook for 10 to 12 minutes. If it is cooking too fast, turn down the heat.

- Remove the lid and, using a hot pad, lift up one side of the casserole to allow any juices to flow to the opposite side. Baste the cooking vegetables with the juices. You may have to move some of the vegetables aside.

- Raise the heat slightly to medium-low. Cook uncovered for about 12 to 15 minutes. Baste the vegetables a few more times as they cook. The liquid will almost evaporate. When it does, turn off the heat and serve.

- Ratatouille can be served hot or cold and is delicious either way.

Scalloped Potatoes
Gratin Dauphinois

From the town of Grenoble in the French Alps comes this famous potato dish. There are many versions of scalloped potatoes, but there is only one *gratin dauphinois*. Try it served with roast chicken (page 60) or as a vegetable main dish.

Serves 4

Ingredients

4 or 5 Idaho potatoes (about 2 pounds)

1 ½ cups whole milk

¼ cup heavy cream

2 ½ tablespoons butter

1 ½ teaspoons salt

¼ teaspoon freshly ground black pepper

¼ teaspoon freshly ground nutmeg

½ cup grated Swiss cheese

On your mark, get set, cook!

- Preheat the oven to 375°F.

- Wash, peel, and slice the potatoes in half lengthwise. Lay a potato half flat side down and cut into ¼-inch slices. Repeat with the remaining potatoes. Measure 6 cups and set aside.

- Measure the milk and cream, combine them in a small saucepan, and place on low heat.

- Butter the sides and bottom of a 3- to 4-quart ovenproof baking dish with 1 tablespoon of the butter. Cut the remaining 1 ½ tablespoons butter into small chunks and set aside.

- Lay the sliced potatoes in the baking dish in overlapping layers. Season the layers with the salt and pepper.

- When the milk and cream come to a boil, add the nutmeg and pour over the potatoes.

- Sprinkle on the grated cheese and dot with the butter.

- Wipe clean any splashes on the rim of the baking dish. Bake the gratin for 1 hour 10 minutes, or until the top is crusted and lightly golden brown. Serve hot.

Glazed Carrots
Carottes Glacées

The French have created many of the world's favorite vegetable dishes, and this recipe from Vichy, in central France, is just one example. Thanks to the versatility of French cooking, this ideal carrot recipe goes beautifully with chicken, fish, or pork and is also perfect just by itself. Once you prepare glazed carrots, with their touch of buttery sweetness, don't be surprised if they're asked for again and again.

Serves 6

Ingredients

10 to 12 carrots (about 2 pounds)

bottled spring water or tap water

5 tablespoons butter

2 tablespoons sugar

1 teaspoon salt

2 to 4 tablespoons chopped fresh flat-leaf parsley

On your mark, get set . . .

- You will want to find carrots that are similar in size. Wash, trim, and peel the carrots, being careful not to remove too much of the carrot skin. Cut the carrots into quarters and then into 2-inch pieces. If the carrots are small and very fresh, leave them unpeeled and gently wash the skins to remove any dirt, then cut in half.

- Place the carrots in a 4-quart saucepan and add the water to just cover about ¼ inch over the carrots.

Cook!

- Bring to a simmer on low heat and cook for about 4 to 5 minutes. Remove a carrot and taste it after it has cooled a bit. It should still be a little underdone.

- Add the butter, sugar, and salt to the saucepan.

- Raise the heat to medium-high and boil rapidly until the liquid has evaporated. This will take another 4 to 5 minutes. Don't

leave the pan unattended or the carrots may burn. Shake the
pan to help glaze the carrots.

- Add the chopped parsley and give the pan a final shake.
  Serve immediately.

Desserts

Cream puffs with ice cream
and chocolate sauce.

Cherry Cake
Clafoutis aux Cerises

This classic cake from Languedoc in the south of France is very popular when cherries are in season. The recipe is easy to make, so it is the perfect finish to any meal. Not cherry season in your neighborhood? You can prepare it with frozen or canned cherries and it will be just as delightful.

Serves 6

Ingredients

FILLING

½ tablespoon butter

2 tablespoons all-purpose flour

1 ½ pounds fresh cherries, or 2 ½ to 3 cups canned or
   frozen Bing or dark sweet cherries

BATTER

1 ½ cups whole milk

⅓ cup sugar

3 eggs

2 teaspoons vanilla extract

⅔ cup all-purpose flour

SAUCE

1 cup reserved liquid from the canned cherries

2 tablespoons cherry or raspberry preserves

¼ cup cold water

On your mark . . .

- Preheat the oven to 350°F.

- Butter a 5- to 6-cup baking dish or cake pan and dust with 2 tablespoons flour. Tip the dish back and forth to completely cover the entire surface with flour. Invert the dish and tap out any excess flour. Set the dish aside.

- If you are using fresh cherries, wash them and remove the stems. Pit the cherries, using a cherry pitter or small sharp knife. Do this over a bowl to catch any juices that might escape.

- If using canned cherries, drain them and reserve the liquid. Place a couple of layers of paper towels on the counter and carefully pour the drained cherries onto them. Place another sheet of paper towels on top and dry the cherries by rolling them back and forth between the layers.

- If using frozen cherries, there is no need to thaw them; just add 10 minutes to the baking time.
- Measure 2 ½ to 3 cups cherries and put them in a clean bowl.

Get set . . .

- Add the batter ingredients to the jar of a blender in the order in which they are listed. Place the lid on the jar securely. Blend at high speed for 1 minute.

- To do this by hand, place the ingredients in a large bowl and blend well with a spoon or whisk.

Cook!

- Spread the cherries evenly across the bottom of the baking dish.
- Gently pour the batter over the cherries.
- Bake on the middle rack of the oven for 50 to 60 minutes, or until the top turns golden brown and the center of the cake is firm. Let the cake rest while you prepare the sauce.
- Pour the reserved liquid from the canned cherries or any juices that accumulated from the fresh cherries into a small saucepan.
- Add the cherry or raspberry preserves and the water and mix well.
- Bring to a boil on medium-high heat. Reduce to simmer and cook for 3 to 4 minutes.
- Bring the sauce to the table in a small serving bowl and let your guests spoon it on the cake slices.
- This cake is delicious topped with whipped cream (page 87) or served just as it is, warm from the oven.

Cream Puffs with Ice Cream and Chocolate Sauce
Profiteroles

Cream puffs are magic. Just wait until you combine the next two recipes to create this famous dessert. Cream puffs filled with French vanilla ice cream and topped with chocolate sauce are what the French call *profiteroles*, but you will call them perfection! First make the cream puff dough and then the chocolate sauce. This is a dessert that will receive a standing ovation.

Makes 12 cream puffs

Ingredients

1 stick unsalted butter (8 tablespoons) plus
   1 ½ teaspoons

1 cup all-purpose flour plus a little extra for dusting

½ teaspoon salt

1 cup water

4 large eggs (not extra-large or jumbo)

1 quart French vanilla ice cream or 1 recipe
   whipped cream (page 87)

1 recipe chocolate sauce (page 86)

On your mark, get set . . .

- Preheat the oven to 400°F.

- Lightly butter a large baking sheet with 1 ½ teaspoons of the butter and dust with a tablespoon or so of the flour. Shake the baking sheet back and forth until the entire surface is coated with flour. Avoid touching the coated surface. Turn the sheet over and tap out the excess flour. Set the baking sheet aside.

- Measure 1 cup flour and ½ teaspoon salt and set aside.

Cook!

- Add the water, 1 stick butter, and salt to a medium-size saucepan, and place on low heat. Bring to a soft boil and cook until the butter has melted.

- Remove the pan from the heat, add the flour all at once, and stir very well with a wooden spoon for about a minute to make sure all the flour is mixed in.

- Place the pan back on the stove and turn the heat to medium. Continue to cook and stir for another 2 minutes. You will see a light film form on the bottom of the pan as you stir. Remove the pan from the heat.

- Pour the dough into a large bowl. Let it cool for about a minute.

- Add 1 egg and beat it into the mixture with an electric hand mixer on low speed. When it is completely mixed in, add another egg and mix in.

- Continue with the third egg and then the fourth. The last egg that is added should bring the dough together into a shiny yellow dough.

- To make the cream puffs: Use two tablespoons, one to scoop the dough and one to push the dough off onto the baking sheet in 12 rounded spoonfuls. Space the spoonfuls of dough about 3 inches apart. Give the tops a little tap to help round them.

- Bake for 40 minutes, or until puffed and golden. Remove the sheet from the oven and, with the tip of a sharp knife, pierce the cream puffs. This will allow the air to escape and dry the insides.

- Return the cream puffs to the oven and bake for another 10 minutes. Let cool completely.

- To serve: Cut each cream puff in half and place the bottom halves on 12 individual serving plates.

- Place 1 scoop French vanilla ice cream or whipped cream in the center of each half. Top with the other half of the cream puff.

- Spoon 1 tablespoon warm chocolate sauce over the filled cream puffs. Serve immediately.

Chocolate Sauce
Sauce au Chocolat

Can one ever say enough about the joys of chocolate? The French have found many delicious ways to use this dark, rich sauce, but none better than as the finishing touch on cream puffs (page 84). Chocolate sauce will keep for up to a week in the refrigerator, but who ever heard of it lasting that long?

Serves 6

Ingredients

½ cup water

3 tablespoons sugar

6 ounces semisweet chocolate

2 tablespoons unsalted butter

¼ cup cold whole milk

1 teaspoon vanilla extract

On your mark, get set, cook!

- Put the water and sugar in a heavy-bottomed 2-quart saucepan and bring to a boil on medium heat. Stir frequently to dissolve the sugar.

- Turn off the heat. Add the chocolate and butter and continue to stir until the sauce is smooth.

- Add the milk and vanilla and combine until the sauce is all the same color.

- Serve warm over cream puffs or ice cream.

Whipped Cream
Crème Chantilly

The French are very clever at turning simple things into the spectacular, and this lightly sweetened whipped cream is a delicious example. This easy recipe is perfect for filling cream puffs (page 84) or serving on top of cherry cake (page 82).

Serves 6

Ingredients

1 cup heavy cream

⅓ cup confectioners' sugar

1 teaspoon vanilla extract

On your mark, get set, whip!

- Place a 2 ½- to 3-quart stainless steel bowl and the beaters to an electric hand mixer in the freezer for 10 minutes to chill completely. Make sure the heavy cream is also very cold.

- Pour the cream into the bowl and beat on high speed with the electric hand mixer. Rotate the bowl and move the beaters in a circle as you whip the cream. This will help mix in lots of air as the cream thickens. It will take about 3 to 4 minutes for the cream to thicken properly, so be patient. You will know it's ready when you see ridges from the beaters on the surface of the cream and soft peaks have formed.

- Turn off the mixer and lift the beaters out of the bowl. If the cream clings to the beaters in soft clouds, it is done; if not, continue beating for another minute.

- After the cream has whipped, add the confectioners' sugar with a flour sifter or hand strainer, gently shaking it over the bowl.

- Add the vanilla and gently fold in the sugar and vanilla with a rubber spatula.

- Keep the whipped cream chilled until ready to serve.

Chef's Tip

Be careful when beating cream not to overwhip it, or you will end up with butter. Turn off the mixer and check the cream now and then as you whip it. You can prepare the cream up to 1 hour before you serve it and it will keep its shape. Remember to cover it with plastic wrap and put it in the refrigerator.

BAKING PAN

SOUFFLÉ DISH

COLANDER

COOKIE SHEETS

CUTTING BOARD

CHERRY PITTER

FOOD PROCESSOR

FOUR-SIDED GRATER

KNIVES, ASSORTED

LADLE

FLOUR SIFTER

ROASTING PAN

ELECTRIC MIXER

MIXING BOWL

MEAT THERMOMETER

SALAD SPINNER

SAUCEPANS WITH LIDS, ASSORTED SIZES

SKILLETS

METAL SLOTTED SPOON

ROLLING PIN

STOCKPOT

STRAINER

TONGS

WHISK

Apple Cider

This is a juice made by pressing and straining a variety of sweet fresh apples. Cider is different from apple juice because it is fermented and generally less filtered and has a stronger apple flavor. Make sure the cider you use is pasteurized.

Bacon

Thick-cut smoked bacon is recommended for the recipes in this book.

Butter

French butter is made from cream and is usually unsalted. American butter comes unsalted (sweet) or salted. If you are more familiar with salted butter, use it for the recipes in this book.

Chives

A member of the onion family, chives taste best when fresh and not dried. Their flavor is more delicate than onions. Chives also make a colorful garnish.

Cream, Heavy

There are different grades of cream ranging from light to heavy, depending on the fat content. Heavy cream is at least 35 percent fat. When buying cream, look for the "sell by" date furthest from the day you purchase it. If possible, avoid buying ultra-pasteurized cream, which can be hard to whip. To successfully whip cream, it is very important to chill the beaters, bowl, and the cream thoroughly before starting.

Dijon Mustard

The city of Dijon in central France is famous for its mustard. Made from three different seeds from the cabbage family, Dijon mustard is pale yellow and full flavored. After you open a jar of mustard, keep it in the refrigerator and it will last several months.

Garlic

Garlic is a member of the onion family and is a valuable flavor maker in French cooking. When you purchase garlic, look for large bulbs that are hard and solid. Inside the bulb are cloves. To use the cloves, first separate them from the bulb. With the flat side of a knife, give them a good whack, then remove the white paperlike skin and cut off the dark tip. The cloves can be chopped into small pieces, mashed, or cut into thin slices. A garlic press is a great way to extract flavor from the cloves. Many nutritionists believe that garlic has great health benefits because it is rich in minerals. The world is separated into two groups of people: those who love garlic and those who don't. Which are you?

Gruyère Cheese

Gruyère is the best known and most highly regarded of all Swiss cheeses. Chefs enjoy it as a versatile cooking cheese because of its nutty flavor and its firm texture, which makes it easy to grate. Both France and Switzerland have different versions of Gruyère, either of which will work very well for the recipes in this book. Swiss cheese is a good substitute.

Niçoise Olives

Niçoise olives are small and black with pits and come from Nice, in the south of France. They are cured in saltwater, or brine, for up to six months. Niçoise olives can usually be found in specialty food stores. Black olives, either Greek or Italian, are a good substitute.

Nutmeg

This spice is native to Indonesia. If used in moderation, it gives dishes a warm, soft flavor. But be careful! Nutmeg can be an overpowering flavor, so don't overdo it. It is best to buy it whole and grate only what you need for your recipe. Store it sealed in a glass jar and it will keep a long time.

Olive Oil, Extra-Virgin

Olive oil is called "extra virgin" if it has been obtained from the first pressing of the olives without the use of chemicals and has low acidity (less than 1 percent). It also has great flavor. Cold-pressed extra-virgin olive oil is regarded as the best of the extra-virgin oils. If the oil is "cold-pressed," that means the olives were pressed without heat, so the oil keeps its flavor. In salad dressings, the flavor of good olive oil will enhance any salad you make. It is important to note that extra-virgin oil can be expensive and so you must consider your budget when buying it. Keep olive oil away from bright sunlight and stored in cool temperatures.

Paprika

Paprika is a spice made from dried sweet red peppers. It is usually added to a recipe not only for its flavor but also for its appealing red color.

Parsley, Flat-Leaf

This variety of parsley is preferable for cooking because it has more flavor than curly-leaf parsley. Look for bright green leaves and stems that are not wilted or shriveled. Be sure you don't make a common mistake and buy fresh cilantro, a similar-looking herb. Wash the parsley before you use it, and chop it, using only the leaves to get the best flavor.

Plums, Dried

Prunes are dried plums. The natural sweetness makes them a flavorful addition to French recipes. When shopping for dried plums, look for those that are minimally processed, pitted, and don't have large amounts of chemical additives.

Port Salut Cheese

A semi-soft cheese made from cow's milk. Trappist Monks first made the cheese in the nineteenth century in the Brittany region of France. It is still produced today and can be found in the cheese section of your supermarket or in specialty cheese stores. The appealing mild flavor and creamy texture is probably why the cheese is still popular with cheese lovers. It must be kept refrigerated.

Shallots

These delicate, small bulbs come from the onion family. Their flavor is much softer than garlic, but their appearance is similar. The flavor of a shallot is released when it is cooked. Shallots should be stored in a cool, dry place out of the sun. They will remain fresh for about three to four weeks after you purchase them.

Thyme

This herb is frequently used in French cooking, particularly in the south of France. The leaves can be used fresh or dried.

Tomatoes

There is no doubt that tomatoes are an ingredient in a great deal of French cooking. When shopping for fresh tomatoes, look for a nice rich red color and avoid fruits with spots or bruises. When you bring them home, keep them away from the heat. Never put fresh tomatoes in the refrigerator. The cold will destroy their flavor and texture.

Turbot

This fish is most commonly found in the waters of the North Sea, an arm of the Atlantic just north of France. It has a firm texture and delicate flavor. If turbot is not available, look for cod, haddock, red snapper, or monkfish.

Vinegar

Apple cider vinegar is made from fermented apple juice. It has a light taste and is used a lot in the cooking of Normandy. Balsamic vinegar is available in many grades, and prices can range from inexpensive to very costly. The price and quality are determined by the age of the vinegar and where it originated. Inexpensive balsamic will work quite well for the recipes in this book. Red wine vinegar is very popular in France and has a deep, rich flavor. Look for red wine vinegar that is bright red and not cloudy.

Walnut Oil

Nutty flavored oil made from pressing walnuts meats. When shopping for walnut oil keep your budget in mind as it can be expensive. Walnut oil should be stored in a cool, dry place and out of sunlight for up to 3 months. It is recommended to store the oil in the refrigerator to prevent it from spoiling. Allow it to come to room temperature before using it.

Find Out More/Metric Conversion Chart

Books

Abramson, Julia. *Food Culture In France* (Food Culture Around the World). Westport, CT: Greenwood, 2006.

Conboy, Fiona and Roseline Ngcheong-Lum. *France* (Welcome to My Country). Tarrytown, NY: Marshall Cavendish Benchmark, 2011.

Websites

French Food and Cook: Cuisine and Recipes from France

http://www.ffcook.com
Offers authentic French menus and recipes, tips and tools, and cooking insights.

Discover France

http://www.discoverfrance.net
Contains a wealth of information about French culture, history, and language.

Metric Conversion Chart You can use the chart below to convert from U.S. measurements to the metric system.

Weight
1 ounce = 28 grams
½ pound (8 ounces) = 227 grams
1 pound = .45 kilogram
2.2 pounds = 1 kilogram

Liquid volume
1 teaspoon = 5 milliliters
1 tablespoon = 15 milliliters
1 fluid ounce = 30 milliliters
1 cup = 240 milliliters (.24 liter)
1 pint = 480 milliliters (.48 liter)
1 quart = .95 liter

Length
¼ inch = .6 centimeter
½ inch = 1.25 centimeters
1 inch = 2.5 centimeters

Temperature
100°F = 40°C
110°F = 45°C
212°F = 100°C (boiling point of water)
350°F = 180°C
375°F = 190°C
400°F = 200°C
425°F = 220°C
450°F = 235°C

(To convert temperatures in Fahrenheit to Celsius, subtract 32 and multiply by .56)

Index

Chef Matthew Locricchio knows a thing or two about cooking. What sets this chef apart from other talented professionals in his field is his knack for imparting this culinary wisdom to children. Matthew was born in Michigan and into a restaurant and catering family, and has spent most of his life in the food industry. Along with his years of training as a chef and his numerous books on cooking, Matthew has made guest appearances on Martha Stewart Radio, *Everyday Food* to talk about his unique approach to getting kids interested in cooking. He has also been heard on *The Faith Middleton Show: Food Schmooze*, on National Public Radio (NPR), and seen on WGN TV, *Lunch Break*, in Chicago.

Matthew's award-winning *The 2nd International Cookbook for Kids* followed up on his earlier *The International Cookbook for Kids*, and, much like the first book, is full of delicious, kid-friendly recipes from around the world.

Also a playwright and actor, Matthew has worked in numerous commercials, soap operas, films, and television shows. Chef Locricchio has been a guest instructor at The Institute of Culinary Education in New York City and Stonewall Kitchen in York, Maine. He guest lectures in the series "Adventures in the Global Kitchen for Kids and Families" at The American Museum of Natural History in New York City.

His brand new *Teen Cuisine*, with spectacular photos by James Beard Winner, James Peterson, was released October 1, 2010. He is currently writing a follow-up with a vegetarian cookbook.

More information about Matthew Locricchio can be found at his website: www.cookbooksandkids.com or www.teencuisinebooks.com